SELECTED POEMS OF MERVYN PEAKE

MERVYN PEAKE

SELECTED POEMS

FABER AND FABER

First published in 1972
First published in this edition 1975
by Faber and Faber Limited
3 Queen Square London WC1
Reprinted 1977
Printed in Great Britain by
Unwin Brothers Limited, Old Woking
All rights reserved

ISBN 0 571 10709 5 (Faber Paperbacks)
ISBN 0 571 09815 0 (hard bound edition)

© 1972 Maeve Peake

Contents

Satan 7

Swallow the Sky 8

In Crazy Balance 9

Out of the Chaos of my Doubt 10

Victoria Station. 6.58 p.m. 11

Coarse as the Sun is Blatant 12

Victims 13

We are the Haunted People 14

A Reverie of Bone 15

That Lance of Light 23

When God Pared his Fingernails 24

Conceit 25

And I Thought You Beside Me 26

Heads Float About Me 27

London 1941 28

The Spadesmen 29

The Time has Come for more than Small Decisions 30

Rather than a Little Pain 31

Is there no Love can Link Us? 32

Onetime my Notes would Dance 33

El Greco 34

Caliban 35

Suddenly, Walking along the Open Road 36

The Modelles 37

Thunder the Christ of it 38

As a Great Town Draws the Eccentrics in 39

The Vastest Things are those We may not Learn 40

When Tiger-men Sat their Mercurial Coursers 41

At Times of Half-light 42

If Trees gushed Blood 43

No Difference 44

Robert Frost 45

To Maeve 46

Some of the poems in this selection have been published before: 'Satan', 'London 1941', 'The Spadesmen', 'Rather than a Little Pain', 'You Walk Unaware' ('To Maeve') in *Shapes and Sounds* (Chatto and Windus, 1941); 'Victims', 'We are the Haunted People', 'A Reverie of Bone', 'When God Pared his Fingernails', 'Conceit', 'And I Thought You Beside Me', 'Heads Float About Me', 'The Time has Come . . .', 'El Greco', 'As a Great Town Draws the Eccentrics in' in *A Reverie of Bone* (Bertram Rota, 1967); 'Caliban', 'The Vastest Things are those We may not Learn', 'When Tiger-men Sat their Mercurial Coursers', 'At Times of Half-light' in *The Glassblowers* (Eyre and Spottiswood, 1950).

Satan

Sickened by virtue he rebelled and cried
For all things horrible to be his bride

For through the hot red tides of sin move such
Fish as lose radiance at virtue's touch.

Should he reform and vomit up his evil ?
It would not only be that his spiked devil
Would be dethroned, but also, amid groans
Those swarming hues that make his joints their homes.

Swallow the Sky

Swallow the sky: chew up the stars
And munch the wind,

For it's on fire with indigestible glory.
The wild pips of the globe bring, in the end
Nothing but torture, but gorge on, my friend,
Swallow the moon, that hump-backed thing,
Your story . . .

Your story and the story of the world
The dread of the cold Universe itself
Sings in the heart-bone high:
Gulp the wild globe and spit it out again
Breaking apart the image of your pain
Swallow the sky!

In Crazy Balance

In crazy balance at the edge of time
Our spent days turn to cloud behind today—
And all tomorrow is a prophet's dream—
This moment only rages endlessly
And prime
Is always the long moment of decay

Out of the Chaos of my Doubt

Out of the chaos of my doubt
And the chaos of my art
I turn to you inevitably
As the needle to the pole
Turns . . . as the cold brain to the soul
Turns in its uncertainty;

So I turn and long for you;
So I long for you, and turn
To the love that through my chaos
Burns a truth,
And lights my path.

Victoria Station. 6.58 p.m.

Sudden, beneath the pendant clock arose
Out of the drab and artificial ground
A horse with wings of scarlet, and pale flowers
Glimmered upon his forehead, while around

His neck and mane like wreaths of incense streamed
Young hosts of stars, and as his eyes burned proud,
The men with black umbrellas stood and stared
And nudged each other and then laughed aloud.

Coarse as the Sun is Blatant

Coarse as the sun is blatant, the high spinach—
Coloured elms, the lawns a yellow matting
Of tired grass, disgust me and the netting
Of summer boughs that creak at every touch.

Of this hot breeze distract me; live apart,
And bring no love to me from other lands,
From other countries, other fields: my hands
Are empty as my blind lop-sided heart!

Lop-sided, for self pity like a curse
Turns all I see to ugliness: the lawns
A wilderness for lack of unicorns fades
The elm a tower for birds of paradise.

Nature! I hate you for you scorch my brain
And make me see my weakness yet again.

Victims

They had no quiet and smoothed sheets of death
To fold them and no pillows whiter than the wings
Of childhood's angels.
There was no hush of love. No silence flowered
About them, and no bland, enormous petals
Opened with stillness. Where was lavender
Or gentle light? Where were the coverlets
Of quiet? Or white hands to hold their bleeding
Claws that grabbed horribly for child or lover?
In twisting flames their twisting bodies blackened,
For History, that witless chronicler
Continued writing his long manuscript.

We are the Haunted People

We are the haunted people
We, who guess blindly at the seed
That flowers
Into the crimson caption,
Hazarding
The birth of that inflamed
Portentous placard that will lose its flavour
Within an hour,
The while the dark deeds move that gave the words
A bastard birth
And hour by hour
Bursts a new gentian flower
Of bitter savour
We have no power . . . no power . . .
We are the haunted people,
We . . .
The last loose tasselated fringe that flies
Into the cold of aeons from a dark
Dynastic gown.

A Reverie of Bone

I sometimes think about old tombs and weeds
That interwreathe among the bones of Kings
With cold and poisonous berry and black flower:
Or ruminate upon the skulls of steeds,
Frailer than shells, or on those luminous wings
The shoulder blades of Princes of fled power,

Which now the unrecorded sandstorms grind
Into so wraith-like a translucency
Of tissue-thin and aqueous-bone; I ponder
On sun-lit spines and in my reverie find
The arc-ribbed courser and his mount to be
Whiter than sexless lilies and how slender

The spleenful hands can turn: I see the gelid
Twigs of the brittle fingers lie so still
And all the arctic filigree of feet:
The porcelain of the breastbone and the pallid
Ulna as downless as the lyric quill
Of some sky-wandering feather that the sleet

And gusts have stripped of all its clinging hairs:
So that a silver-shred of whiteness wanders
Across the stars until the night winds fail.
O ribs of light! Bright flight, yours are such stairs
As wail at midnight when the sand meanders
Through your cold rungs that sieve the desert gale.

O string the arrogant ribs with spider-twine
Torn from those webs that hold the murderous arms
Of thorn-crazed boughs together, that a gust
May pluck the resonant threads to a white rune
Of memory, a music of fled forms,
An ancient cadence from the ancient dust.

White lyre of ribs, cold cage, white cage curling
How deliberate from the razed spine's pagoda
Spring each way in stilled phalanx, tapering
To the basin'd pelvis and to where the skirling
And cave-cold winds within the skull are louder
Than the pulse-drums at the temples leaping

And your white blades and thin stems interlaced
And freed forever from the oppressive clay.
I watch you glimmer by the dying light
Of my dark brain, as pranked across a waste
Of restless gloom, the sea-froth seems to stay
A moment frozen to the aqueous night.

The heaving sea-hills gulp these sudden chalk-
White markings, as a sand-hill drags the bone
Into as deep a maw, from hour to hour.
For dunes, the sustenance of the hollow stalk,
For waves the silver diet of the lone
And yet gregarious ghostland of the flower.

Cold spectre-flower, that, dying, lifts a sister
To the insatiate surface of the ocean.
The buried stalk, less rapid through the dune
Is no less sure, for the dry heavings muster
The brittle brothers though with tardier motion
They climb their stifling stairways to the moon.

There are no keels for this forgotten ocean,
Not one, for all this ochreous waste: no wave
Feels its hot forehead at the sudden turn
And pressure of a vagrant prow break open,
And there would be no foam of ruth to lave
The wounded comber if it were to happen.

These shipless, corrugated oceans cry
With the false voices of their surface rollers
'We are a fathom shallow: we are breaking
Over a paddler's base,' and the pursed eye
Of the helmsman in a lidded language mutters
'Here lie the shoals! Beware! The waves are flaking!'

Yet the impossible helmsman with his eye
Schooled to the pregnant by-play of great waters
Forgets that waves of repetitive, stumbling shale
Can undulate as though a shelving bay
Lay by, and yet be deep as those cold quarters
Where blind eels sprawl and all the strong lights fail.

Forgets that the misleading breakers are
Curled by the winds and beneath them falls
Depth upon depth to the pulseless places
And in a ship whose mast impales a star
Whose sails drip glass along two skylines, calls
For vigilance while his free keel slices.

The plains remain. The sun, and the chill moon
With taunting freshness circle the old sky
The ancient winds for whom there's no decay.
Is every part of man to slide so soon
Into the namelessness? Ah no, for see
The bone remains and will not burn away.

How still it lies when the thick storm abates
And every grain has settled from the sky.
A lord upon a steed of alabaster
Rides on his side until I ruminate
How lost in the wild desert of the eye
A black horse stumbled northwards to disaster.

Through endless sand: the throats of steed and rider
Coughed out their last before a waterless death
Together lying: they are yet alone.
I glimpse them as they were, less rare, but prouder,
The bright blood coiled around them like a wreath
Of sultry vine that swarms their plinths of bone.

I see you Rider, my imagined rider,
In purple, and the great locks of your hair
Lift in the sunny wind; you cry and swing
The dancing courser upright; you were cruder
Than now, as chill and delicate, your bare
Twin femurs lie astride the scaffolding

Of that which serves the softly pouring sands.
The sunlit arches of your horse's ribs
Are one with yours in that which is more rare
Than pride of carriage, or the grip of hands
Upon a lashing mane, and all the webs
Of veins that branch and throb from sole to hair.

O Prince in purple you are lovelier now,
Your bracelets, curls and lips and eyelids gone,
Your studded crown, your quick imperious breath,
Your heart that some gaunt eagle far ago
Carried aloft beneath a desert moon
To the matted eyrie of its ghastly kith.

You are more lovely now: desireless
Your bones comply with every feckless wind
That shifts the pouring hills from place to place.
Freed from the tumult of the blood's excess,
And the insistent cloudland of the blind,
Slow cumulous of flesh. The breast, the face,

The thigh and all the members choked your white
Reality, your stern, ancestral joy
Changeless beneath the flux of tidal clay.
Your perfectness reflects the moon at night
While bones of lords and mendicants, deploy
Your fleshless journeys through the night and day.

What is more exquisite than to be free
Of all that presses on the crying core
Of the long bones, that now so nakedly
Can hear the desert winds along the scree,
How loud they are that were so drugged before,
By the dumb bullion of the shrouding clay.

Queens in their tombs are mouthed by the furred lips
Of humid plants, or, stretched upon stone shelves
Of granite, where the sandy sunlight fingers,
How ruminatively with hazy fingertips
High tiers of skeletons and skulls revolve
Among the motes where the dank lizard lingers.

For these the pride of palaces, a tomb
But for each bone that whitens in the dark
A million blossom on the desertlands,
The skulls of nomads echo in the gloom
To the lions' throated thunder or the bark
Of jackals as they scour the shadowy sands.

And yet not only in the brain's gray spaces
Which, at the imagination's astral touch
Flare into focus, all horizon's failing . . .
Not only through the wastes of thought uprises
A ghosted mountain lit by the full torch
Of a sailing moon that never ceases sailing

Not only in the brain, nor in the heart
Nor out of love, nor through untethered fancy
Is that cold mountain littered with the white
Residue of the dead, as though its bright
Steep sides were dusted with dry leprosy
Nor any other death-engendered sight

Which I envisage in deserted places—
But, in the ruthless regions of what's true
And I can only hope to grasp the worth
From vast and leaping landscapes, which Time passes
Beneath my pen-nib as it trails the blue
Thread of my thought behind each glimpse of truth.

This is no figment but a glimpse of all
That is so beautiful in the long dead,
Those delicate carvings that deny the night.
Over the burning scarp a prophet's skull
Revolves before the winds, its lengthened shade
Cruising before it as it rolls through sunlight.

All this is true; this hand that props my forehead
Is no more real than those hands of frost
That lie in myriads like a silver choir
Of endless gesture, eloquent though dead.
Hands yearning, voiceless through their quilts of dust,
O skulls, blades and ribs made white in the long sunfire.

O passionless, amoral, unearthly whiteness
Emptied of ardour like a thought of crystal
Scoring a circle in the air of time:
Closer to darkness is this loveless lightness
Than to the wanest breath of colour. All
That is most ultimate and clear: the prime

And essence of a dream that flowering, loses
Its colour-tinctured parts in finding climax
And consummation in a spectral land,
Vaster than arctic, rarer than where cruises
The frigate moon, is your domain that works
Its magic in the thighbone on the sand.

As bleached and scrupulous as that stern linen
Da Vinci laid forever underneath
The isolation of the unfingered loaves
The desolation of the untasted wine,
The thirteen double islands from the earth,
Stiff, icebound and estranged from vines and sheaves

Show with their pool and crust how pure is flax,
How cold it is and how immaculate
And close it is at the supper, charged and lorn
To the asceticism of the stern stalk
Of hollow bone that the same master sought.
Blanched, holy whiteness that continues on.

And every dawn the scything sunlight sweeps
Upon the strewn mementoes of the token
Epochs of passion; on the breastbone of
A suicide; or the rich steeps
The jawbone of a merchant, or the broken
Rib of an alchemist protrudes above

A knoll that by the noonday shall have slid
Under the wind's compulsion to a vale,
And dragged the stringless bow sand-fathoms under,
And all is changed, the hills as hot as blood
Have given place to corrugated, pale
And ash-gray tracts that have thrown up fresh plunder

From the sterile torpor of the desert's womb;
So that, across the desolate plains are littered
Fresh relics of incongruous dynasties—
Bones, that when sunrise flowered through the gloom
Were sunless, glitter now, where they lie scattered,
Scudding across the melancholy land.

A reverie of bone the beautiful!
Science must strike its colours at the white
Articulate splendour, be it peace or war.
Enough of wonder and of death. Set sail
For other waters of less deathly light
Where life and breath as vast and splendid are.

I sometimes think about old tombs and weeds
That interwreathe among the bones of Kings
With cold and poisonous berry and black flower:
Or ruminate upon the skulls of steeds,
Frailer than shells, or on those luminous wings
The shoulder blades of Princes of fled power.

That Lance of Light

That lance of light that slid across the dark
To disappear a moment later, when
A cloud like a great haystack with its angry
Hair awry devoured it and then spat
It out like the barbed war-head of a lyric,
Sang earthward, and a million light-years later
Pierced the green dark of a tall weed-hung vessel,
And in a cup of honey-coloured light
Hissed at the impact.

When God Pared his Fingernails

When God had pared his fingernails
He found that only nine
Lay on that golden tablet
Where the silver curves recline
When they have left his hands of cloud
And gleam in one lone line.

'Rebellion!' cried the Angels 'Where
Has flown the Nail of Sin?'
I saw it running through cold skies
Last night; so fierce and thin
A silver shape, that ran
And ran—it was the moon.

Conceit

I heard a winter tree in song
Its leaves were birds, a hundred strong;
When all at once it ceased to sing,
For every leaf had taken wing.

And I Thought You Beside Me

And I thought you beside me
How rare and how desperate
And your eyes were wet
And your face as still
As the body of a leveret
On a tranced hill
But my thought belied me
And you were not there
But only the trees that shook
Only a storm that broke
Through the dark air.

Heads Float About Me

Heads float about me; come and go, absorb me;
Terrify me that they deny the nightmare
That they should be, defy me;
And all the secrecy; the horror
Of truth, of this intrinsic truth
Drifting, ah God, along the corridors
Of the world; hearing the metal
Clang; and the rolling wheels.
Heads float about me haunted
By solitary sorrows.

London 1941

Half masonry, half pain; her head
From which the plaster breaks away
Like flesh from the rough bone, is turned
Upon a neck of stones; her eyes
Are lid-less windows of smashed glass,
Each star-shaped pupil
Giving upon a vault so vast
How can the head contain it?

The raw smoke
Is inter-wreathing through the jaggedness
Of her sky-broken panes, and mirror'd
Fires dance like madmen on the splinters.

All else is stillness save the dancing splinters
And the slow inter-wreathing of the smoke.

Her breasts are crumbling brick where the black ivy
Had clung like a fantastic child for succour
And now hangs draggled with long peels of paper,
Fire-crisp, fire-faded awnings of limp paper
Repeating still their ghosted leaf and lily.

Grass for her cold skin's hair, the grass of cities
Wilted and swaying on her plaster brow
From winds that stream along the streets of cities:

Across a world of sudden fear and firelight
She towers erect, the great stones at her throat,
Her rusted ribs like railings round her heart;
A figure of dry wounds—of winter wounds—
O mother of wounds; half masonry, half plain.

The Spadesmen

There is no lack of light and singing limbs
Of throats and ribs and all the naked gear
That holds the quick breath in; there is no fear
That these will fail them and dissolve like dreams,

Now that each grave is scooped, each cross is varnished;
The robes of purple from the factory
Hang from the branches of gethsemane—
The coffins gleam and all the brass is burnished.

They have supplied the judas and the flails:
The ten-a-minute barbed-wire crown-of-thorns
Are in construction and a million pawns
Are ear-marked for the fever and the nails.

They have prepared the swabs of vinegar,
Long tears for cheer-bones and a load of lime.
The spadesmen have been working overtime
To raise so high a mound of golgotha.

The Time has Come for more than Small Decisions

The time has come for more than small decisions.
I have my battleground no less than nations:
I have great traitors in the populous clay:
I am, no less than Albion, at war—
For while she struggles I must force my way
Into a land where sharper outlines are.

Before man's bravery I bow my head;
More so when valour is unnatural
And fear, a bat between the shoulder-blades
Flaps its cold webs—but I am ill at ease
With propaganda glory, and the lies
Of statesmen and the lords of slippery trades.

O let me find a way of thought that cuts
An angry line dividing this from that
And scours the soft winds that have no court.

May 1941

Rather than a Little Pain

Rather than a little pain, I would be thief
To the organ-chords of grief
That toll through me
With a burial glory.

Wherefore my searching dust
If not to breathe the Gust
Of every quarter
Before I scatter,

And to divine
The lit or hooded Ghost, and take for mine
The double pulse; so come
Forth from your midnight tomb

Cold grief
I would be thief
Of you
Until my bones breed hemlock through and through.

Is there no Love can Link Us?

Is there no thread to bind us—I and he
Who is dying now, this instant as I write
And may be cold before this line's complete?

And is there no power to link us—I and she
Across whose body the loud roof is falling?

Or the child, whose blackening skin
Blossoms with hideous roses in the smoke?

Is there no love can link us—I and they?
Only this hectic moment? This fierce instant
Striking now
Its universal, its uneven blow?

There is no other link. Only this sliding
Second we share: this desperate edge of now.

Onetime my Notes would Dance

Onetime my notes would dance to any theme.
They are not dancing for nothing dances
When my heart stands rigid

I had a reed but I have snapped its body
Across my brain. I danced; I had a fiddle

But since I heard all instruments together
Surge up the blood red spiral to the sunlight
I have smashed my fiddle.

What once I would have sung I now deny
For I have heard the organ chords of grief
Break loose and cry from wars
Arising out of death's dark orchestra.

Oh I have crushed my bright notes underfoot
Like crystals in the dirt—and of all that's me
   Only my tears move.

El Greco

They spire terrific bodies into heaven,
Tall saints enswathed in a tempestuous flare
Of frozen draperies that twist through air,
Of dye incredible, from rapture thieven,
And heads set steeply skyward brittle carven
Pale upon coiling cloud in regions rare.
Their beauty, ice-like, shrills, and everywhere
A metal music sounds, cold spirit grieven.

So drives the acid nail of coloured pain
Into our vulnerable wood earth-rooted,
And sends the red sap racing through the trees
Where slugged it lay—now spun with visions looted
From whining skies, and sharp Gethsmanés
Of hollow light and all the wounds of Spain.

Caliban

As much himself is he as Caliban
Is Caliban or Ariel, Ariel.
I shook with jealousy to see a man
Strut with such bombast to his burial.

Loathing my piebald heart that strikes ambiguous
Chords in my breast,
I watched him spit the bright pips as he stalked
Into the darkness like a golden beast.

Suddenly, Walking along the Open Road

Suddenly, walking along the open road I felt afraid.
I saw the stars and the world below my feet
Became a planet, and I was no longer
In Wiltshire. I was standing
Upon the surface, the edge of a planet
That runs around the sun.
I was in danger.
For all the comfort of the elms, the banal
Normality of houses with their garages, the apparent
Changelessness of the ploughed field on my right—
All was in danger.
A marble spinning through the universe
Wears on its dizzy crust, men, houses, trees
That circle through cavernous aeons, and I was afraid.

The Modelles

In this, the vast absorption, burns the angel.
Strange among rowdy gods, that break the air
Of now, with treacherous eyes and bloody hair
Is clay, his medium, his miracle

Of plastic birth, his lover, his white devil,
His world of silver flesh; the one his hands
Nurture in silence while the tocsin sounds
And Europe loads the gun-gray bird for evil.

Thunder the Christ of it

Thunder the Christ of it. The field is free:
To everyone his choice: that martial fellow,
His mouth cram full of nails squats in a tree:
Gallop you traitors in. Judas in yellow:

While bibles burn, Leviticus and all,
Christ is forgotten in a world of wit:
Soak up the planets in a swab of gall,
This is the day and we must pay for it.

As a Great Town Draws the Eccentrics in

As a great town draws the eccentrics in,
So I am like a city built of clay
Where madmen flourish, for beneath my skin,
In every secret arch or alleyway

That winds about my bones of midnight, they
Lurk in their rags, impatient for the call
To muster at my breastbone, and to cry
For revolution through the capital.

The Vastest Things are those We may not Learn

The vastest things are those we may not learn.
We are not taught to die, nor to be born,
Nor how to burn
With love
How pitiful is our enforced return
To those small things we are the masters of.

When Tiger-men Sat their Mercurial Coursers

When tiger-men sat their mercurial coursers,
Hauled into shuddering arches the proud fibre
Of head and throat, sank spurs, and trod on air—
       I was not there. . . .

When clamorous centaurs thundered to the rain-pools,
Shattered with their fierce hooves the silent mirrors,
When glittering drops clung to their beards and hair—
       I was not there. . . .

When through a blood-dark dawn a man with antlers
Cried, and throughout the day the echoes suffered
His agony and died in evening air—
       I was not there. . . .

At Times of Half-light

It is at times of half-light that I find
Forsaken monsters shouldering through my mind.
If the earth were lamplit I should always be
Found in their company.

Even in sunlight I have heard them clamouring
About the gateways of my brain, with glimmering
Rags about their bruise-dark bodies bound,
And in each brow a ruby like a wound.

If Trees gushed Blood

If trees gushed blood
When they were felled
By meddling man,
And crimson welled

From every gash
His axe can give,
Would he forbear,
And let them live ?

No Difference

There is no difference between night and day
For time is darkness now, halted and null.
The roads of noon lead their abstracted way,
The streets of midnight wander through the Skull.

Darkness and time have fused and formed a circle
Around the little gestures of the clay
And there's no movement but the gusty cycle
Of calendars that tear dark leaves away.

Robert Frost

The great tree creaked and splinters of sharp ice
Broke from the frozen branches in a shower;
I thought of Robert Frost and of his power
With simple words that he can so entice
And wake
To such a startling order; they can bring
Fresh grass up wet against the heart and slake
My English dust with his New England spring.

To Maeve

You walk unaware
Of the slender gazelle
That moves as you move
And is one with the limbs
That you have.

You live unaware
Of the faint, the unearthly
Echo of hooves
That within your white streams
Of clear clay that I love

Are in flight as you turn,
As you stand, as you move,
As you sleep, for the slender
Gazelle never rests
In your ivory grove.